I'D RATHER BE

SAILING

Library of Congress Catalog Card Number: 96-86637

ISBN: 0-8362-2732-8

ATTENTION: SCHOOLS AND BUSINESSES

Andrews and McMeel books are available at quantity discounts with bulk purchase for educational, business, or sales promotional use. For information, please write to: Special Sales Department, Andrews and McMeel, 4520 Main Street, Kansas City, Missouri 64111.

I'D RATHER BE

SAILING

EDITED BY ANNE DEPUE

Andrews and McMeel
A Universal Press Syndicate Company
Kansas City

INTRODUCTION

The weather report comes in. Breezy conditions, sunny skies, calm seas. With these words, a shiver of longing runs through the soul of every sailor. Thoughts turn to the sea, to the rush of wind against the cheek, to invigorating salt smells or the perfume of a lake. The thrilling sensation of slipping through waves grows as the wind picks up and a chorus of halyards beats against the mast, demanding to challenge the elements.

Throughout history, sailing has held forth a magical promise. Whether voyaging to distant new lands or tacking back and forth across a narrow bay, whether alone or with a crew of friends, the sailor finds in the sea freedom and adventure.

"To sail is the thing," wrote Arthur Ransome in his children's classic *Swallows and Amazons*. And just what is that thing? Every sailor knows. It's what the poets say and the pictures show, and everything else, too; it's the joy of casting off and the delight at returning home, and it's all the winds and waves in between. It's the beauty of a boat and the power of the currents, the sound of ratcheting winches and the strain on the wheel; it's the fair breezes and sunsets, the storms and luffing sails. It's the beer in the bar when the race is done, and that moment when you feel you'll never get there. It's what sailors mean when, safe and dry, standing on solid ground, they look at you and say: "I'd rather be sailing."

— Anne Depue

So we beat on, boats against the current, borne back ceaselessly into the past.

—F. Scott Fitzgerald, *The Great Gatsby*

A harbor, even if it is a little harbor, is a good thing, since adventures come into it as well as go out, and the life in it grows strong, because it takes something from the world and has something to give in return.

—SARAH ORNE JEWETT, *COUNTRY BYWAYS*, *RIVER DRIFTWOOD*

It's like standing under a cold shower tearing up five-pound notes.

——EDWARD HEATH, *ON SAILBOAT RACING*

Give a man health and a course to steer, and he'll never stop to trouble about whether he's happy or not.

—GEORGE BERNARD SHAW, *BRASSBOUND'S CONVERSION*

The anchor heaves, the ship swings free,
The sails swell full. To sea, to sea!
—THOMAS LOVELL BEDDOES, *SAILOR'S SONG*

There is nothing, absolutely nothing, half so much worth doing as simply messing about in boats, or with boats. In or out of 'em, it doesn't matter.

—KENNETH GRAHAME, *THE WIND IN THE WILLOWS*

Mothlike in mists, scintillant in the minute
brilliance of cloudless days, with broad bellying sails
they glide to the wind tossing green water
from their sharp prows while over them the crew crawls.

—WILLIAM CARLOS WILLIAMS, *THE YACHTS*

The sea never changes and its works, for all the talk of men,
are wrapped in mystery.

—JOSEPH CONRAD, *TYPHOON*

A wet sheet and a flowing sea,
A wind that follows fast,
And fills the white and rustling sail,
And bends the gallant mast.

—ALLAN CUNNINGHAM, *THE SONGS OF SCOTLAND, ANCIENT AND MODERN*

I find the great thing in this world is not
so much where we stand, as in what
direction we are moving: To reach the port
of heaven, we must sail sometimes with
the wind and sometimes against it, but
we must sail, and not drift, nor lie at anchor.
—OLIVER WENDELL HOLMES, *THE AUTOCRAT AT THE BREAKFAST TABLE*

Give me a spirit that on this life's rough sea
Loves t' have his sails filled with a lusty wind,
Even till his sail-yards tremble, his masts crack,
And his rapt ship run on her side so low
That she drinks water, and her keel plows air.

——GEORGE CHAPMAN, *THE CONSPIRACY AND TRAGEDY OF CHARLES DUKE OF BYRON*

A knot is never "nearly right"; it is either exactly right or it is hopelessly wrong, one or the other; there is nothing in between.

—CLIFFORD ASHLEY, *THE ASHLEY BOOK OF KNOTS*

I must down to the seas again, to the lonely sea and the sky,
And all I ask is a tall ship and a star to steer her by,
And the wheel's kick and the wind's song and
the white sail's shaking,
And a gray mist on the sea's face and a gray dawn breaking.

—JOHN MASEFIELD, *SEA-FEVER*

He who commands the sea has command of everything.

—THEMISTOCLES, FROM *CICERO*

for whatever we lose (like a you or a me)
it's always ourselves we find in the sea.

—E.E. CUMMINGS, *THE SEA*

The fair breeze blew, the white foam flew,
The furrows followed free;
We were the first that ever burst
Into that silent sea.

—SAMUEL TAYLOR COLERIDGE, *THE RIME OF THE ANCIENT MARINER*

⚓

What fates impose, that men must needs abide;
It boots not to resist both wind and tide.
—WILLIAM SHAKESPEARE, *HENRY VI*

The sea hates a coward.

——Eugene O'Neill, *Mourning Becomes Electra: A Trilogy*

He gained a world; he gave that world
Its grandest lesson: Sail On! Sail On!

—JOAQUIN MILLER, *COLUMBUS*

I have seen old ships sail like swans asleep.

——JAMES ELROY FLECKER, *THE OLD SHIPS*

A solitary sail that rises
White in the blue mist on the foam
What is it in far lands it prizes?
What does it leave behind at home?

—MIKHAIL LERMONTOV, *A Sail*

If a man must be obsessed by something, I suppose a boat is as good as anything, perhaps a bit better than most. A small sailing craft is not only beautiful, it is seductive and full of strange promise and the hint of trouble.

—E.B. White, *The Sea and the Wind that Blows*

There is something about boats which makes one feel they are living creatures—each as different from her sisters as human beings are from each other. The very fact that one refers to a boat as "she" shows that since time began men have loved their boats.

—Francis Kinney, *Skene's Elements of Yacht Design*

Choosing a yacht is by no means a simple or straightforward process if one seeks the perfect boat for oneself. Beauty, certainly; seaworthiness, of course; speed, naturally. But should it be the elegant beauty of the 12-meter sloop, whose breathtaking grace is apparent to everybody, or the complex beauty of the fat center-boarder, whose lines require an educated eye to appreciate? Should speed be called for, or are concessions to comfort and sloth worth the sacrifice of speed in light airs? Alas, these are not questions that can be decided in the abstract; and, as when one ponders marriage, they call for a degree of self-knowledge hard to summon up just when it is needed most.

—ARTHUR BEISER, *THE PROPER YACHT*

The desire to build a house is the tired wish of a man content thenceforward with a single anchorage. The desire to build a boat is the desire of youth, unwilling yet to accept the idea of a final resting place. . . . When it comes, the desire to build a boat is one of those that cannot be resisted. It begins as a little cloud on a serene horizon. It ends by covering the whole sky, so that you can think of nothing else. You must build to regain your freedom.

—ARTHUR RANSOME, *RACUNDRA'S FIRST CRUISE*

The wonder is always new that any sane man can be a sailor.

—Ralph Waldo Emerson

Sailing any one of the Seven Seas is a mysterious pleasure, for the fascination and fun of it are so great that they overcome the moments of misfortune and misery we must suffer at sea. We must know heartache to enjoy happiness, and know hunger to enjoy a meal, however good.

—UFFA FOX, *ACCORDING TO UFFA*

To know the laws that govern the winds, and to know that you know them, will give you an easy mind on your voyage around the world; otherwise you may tremble at the appearance of every cloud.

—JOSHUA SLOCOM, *SAILING ALONE AROUND THE WORLD*

Gray-eyed Athena sent them a favorable breeze, a fresh west wind,
singing over the wine-dark sea.

—HOMER, *THE ODYSSEY*

Anyone can hold the helm when the sea is calm.

—PUBLILLIUS SYRUS, *MAXIM 358*

Let your boat of life be light, packed with only what you need: a homely home and simple pleasures, one or two friends, worth the name, someone to love and someone to love you, a cat, a dog, and a pipe or two, enough to eat and enough to wear, and a little more than enough to drink; for thirst is a dangerous thing.

—JEROME K. JEROME, *THREE MEN IN A BOAT*

There is witchery in the sea, its songs and stories, and in the mere sight of a ship, and the sailor's dress . . . the very creaking of a block . . . and many are the boys, in every seaport, who are drawn away, as by an almost irresistible attraction, from their work and schools, and hang about the decks and yards of vessels, with a fondness which, it is plain, will have its way.

—RICHARD HENRY DANA, JR., *TWO YEARS BEFORE THE MAST*

The thrill of sailing and putting out in a boat cannot be expressed in words. It is the feeling of power and the awe of making the wind do your work . . . or putting your strength to the severest test of man and rigging. It is the aesthetic appeal of a beautiful hull and a bleached sail. And it is the quiet noise of water sloshing against the prow as you rest in your berth in the forecastle, absorbing a lifetime of memories.

—ALAN BROWN, *INVITATION TO SAILING*

Sea of strech'd ground-swells,
Sea breathing broad and convulsive breaths,
Sea of the brine of life and of unshovell'd yet always-ready graves,
Howler and scooper of storms, capricious and dainty sea,
I am integral with you, I too am of one phase and of all phases.
—WALT WHITMAN, *SONG OF MYSELF*

We left behind the painted buoy
That tosses at the harbour mouth;
And madly danced our hearts with joy,
As fast we fleeted to the South:
How fresh was every sight and sound
On open main or winding shore!
We knew the merry world was round,
And we might sail for evermore.

—ALFRED LORD TENNYSON, *THE VOYAGE*

I expected every wave would have swallowed us up, and that every time the ship fell down, as I thought, in the trough or hollow of the sea, we should never rise more; and in this agony of mind I made many vows and resolutions, that if it please God here to spare my life this one voyage, if ever I got once my foot upon dry land again, I would go directly home to my father, and never set it into a ship again while I liv'd; that I would take his advice, and never run myself into such miseries as these any more.

——DANIEL DEFOE, *ROBINSON CRUSOE*

O it's I that am the captain of a tidy little ship,
  Of a ship that goes a-sailing on the pond;
And my ship it keeps a-turning all around and all about;
But when I'm a little older, I shall find the secret out
  How to send my vessel sailing on beyond.

—ROBERT LOUIS STEVENSON, *MY SHIP AND I*

Many people develop a kind of love-hate relationship with the spinnaker, and it has often been said that this sail is the easiest to hoist but requires the most courage.

—R. "BUNTY" KING, *SPINNAKER*

If the desire is to sail grandly and the resources are there, it does not do today, any more than during the golden age of the huge J-Boats, to count with progressive dismay the dollars spent.

—WILLIAM F. BUCKLEY, JR., *RACING THROUGH PARADISE*

I have had to pass a considerable portion of my life aboard small craft of various kinds, and after a long and mixed experience of the life, I have come to two very definite conclusions concerning it. One is that life on a small boat in fine weather is the only kind of life worth living. The other is that, in bad weather, it's just plain hell.

—WESTON MARTYR, *THE SOUTHSEAMAN*

The compass may go wrong, the stars never.

—SHIP'S CAPTAIN FROM TONGA, *THE KON-TIKI EXPEDITION*

No man will be a sailor who has contrivance enough to get himself into a jail; for being on a ship is being in a jail, with the chance of being drowned . . . . A man in a jail has more room, better food, and commonly better company.

—SAMUEL JOHNSON

What is it in the sea life which is so powerful in its influence? It is the sense of things done, of things endured, or meanings not understood; the secret of the Deep Silence, which is of eternity, which the heart cannot speak.

—H. WARINGTON SMYTH, *MAST AND SAIL*

For all at last returns to the sea: to Oceanus, the ocean river, like the ever-flowing stream of time, the beginning and the end.

—RACHEL CARSON, *THE SEA AROUND US*

SELECTED BIBLIOGRAPHY

Ashley, Clifford. *The Ashley Book of Knots* (Doubleday, 1944).

Beddoes, Thomas. *The Poetical Works of Thomas Lovell Beddoes* (Dent, 1890).

Beiser, Arthur. *The Proper Yacht* (Macmillan, 1970).

Brown, Alan. *Invitation to Sailing* (Simon & Schuster, 1971).

Buckley, William F., Jr. *Racing Through Paradise* (Random House, 1987).

Carson, Rachel. *The Sea Around Us* (Staples, 1951).

Chapman, George. *The Conspiracy & Tragedy of Charles Duke of Byron* (St. Martin's Press, 1990).

Coleridge, Samuel Taylor. *The Rime of the Ancient Mariner* (Chatto & Windus, 1798).

Conrad, Joseph. *Typhoon* (*Pall Mall Gazette*, January-March 1902).

Cunningham, Allan. *The Songs of Scotland, Ancient and Modern* (1825).

Dana, Richard Henry, Jr. *Two Years Before the Mast* (1869).

Defoe, Daniel. *Robinson Crusoe* (Knopf, 1719).

Fitzgerald, F. Scott. *The Great Gatsby* (Scribners, 1925).

Fox, Uffa. *According to Uffa* (George Newnes, 1960).

Cunningham, Allan. *The Songs of Scotland, Ancient and Modern* (1825).

Dana, Richard Henry, Jr. *Two Years Before the Mast* (1869).

Defoe, Daniel. *Robinson Crusoe* (Knopf, 1719).

Fitzgerald, F. Scott. *The Great Gatsby* (Scribners, 1925).

Fox, Uffa. *According to Uffa* (George Newnes, 1960).

Grahame, Kenneth. *The Wind in the Willows* (Scribners, 1908).

Heyerdahl, Thor. *The Kon-Tiki Expedition* (Allen & Unwin, 1950).

Holmes, Oliver Wendell. *The Autocrat at the Breakfast Table* (New American Library, 1857).

Jerome, Jerome K. *Three Men in a Boat* (Viking, 1978).

King, R. "Bunty." *Spinnaker* (Sail Books, 1981).

Kinney, Francis. *Skene's Elements of Yacht Design* (Dodd, Mead, 1927).

Martyr, Weston. *The Southseaman* (Blackwood, 1926).

Masefield, John. *Salt-water Poems and Ballads* (Macmillan, 1916).

Miller, Joaquin. *The Complete Poetical Works of Joaquin Miller* (Whitaker & Ray, 1897).

O'Neill, Eugene. *Mourning Becomes Electra: A Trilogy* (Vintage, 1931).

Raban, Jonathan. *The Oxford Book of the Sea* (Oxford University Press, 1992).

Slocum, Joshua. *Sailing Alone Around the World* (Dover, 1956).

Smyth, H. Warington. *Mast and Sail* (John Murray, 1906).

Stevenson, Robert Louis. *A Child's Garden of Verse* (1885).

Tennyson, Alfred Lord. *The Complete Poetical Works of Alfred Lord Tennyson* (Houghton Mifflin, 1898).

White, E. B. *The Essays of E.B. White* (Harper Collins, 1963).

Whitman, Walt. *The Complete Poems* (Penguin, 1986).

CREDITS